D1389782

Backpacking Equipment

COMPANION VOLUMES

ADVENTURE CYCLING
in Britain
Tim Hughes

MODERN WATER-SKIING
A Guide for Skiers
and Boat Drivers
R. J. Prytherch

Backpacking Equipment
MAKING IT and USING IT

G.R.Birch

BLANDFORD PRESS
Poole   Dorset

First published 1978

Copyright © 1978 Blandford Press Ltd.
Link House, West Street
Poole, Dorset BH15 1LL

ISBN 0 7137 0875 1

Printed in Great Britain by Unwin Brothers Limited,
The Gresham Press, Old Woking, Surrey

Contents

Publisher's Note

The equipment and clothing described in this book are the result of experiment and testing, adaptation and modification by the author over a period of time and are the product of his original thought. The greatest care has been taken not to infringe patents, but it is possible that similar equipment and clothing for such specific functions have been produced by other persons at some time. Indeed, to show the range available we have illustrated some examples of manufactured equipment and the author and publisher gratefully acknowledge the following manufacturers and suppliers as sources of illustrations: Blacks of Greenock (endpapers); 'Pointfive' (page 26); Robert Saunders Ltd (page 74). All other illustrations are by the author, who emphasizes that in the adventure activity of camping, due care and common sense must be exercised, as in all outdoor activities.

1

An Introduction to Backpacking

What greater joy can there be than to lie in one's tent and watch the moon rise out of a darkling sea off some picturesque headland, or to be camped on a lonely mountain in the early morning amid a silent world bathed in a brilliant sunrise. Such are the incidents one remembers, when the anxieties and stress of modern life become unbearable.

Many people read about camping and backpacking. In the busy city office, factory or high rise flat they daydream of the time—sometime—when they can escape from their artificial surroundings, the noise, the dirty air and the pressure to a more casual tranquil life. Camping, in general, and backpacking in particular offers such people the mental and physical refreshment they require.

The clock means nothing to the backpacker; being fully organised, the only worry is where to camp that night, and when to renew the stock of food. A free agent, the backpacker can travel to places inaccessible to the motorist or tripper—it is true freedom.

No-one should embark on a backpacking venture without some experience in static camping on a site. Those who have never camped before are often deterred by the thought of the high cost of equipment—or have quite an irrational fear of sleeping in a tent, based on lack of knowledge or alarming experiences related by friends or relations who have camped.

In the season, many camping shops offer facilities for holidaymakers to hire tents and equipment, and for those who have never camped before, this is an ideal opportunity to find out if they like it. A holiday such as this will give them the chance to organise the cooking arrangements, to find out if they are warm enough with the sleeping bags, and give them practice in pitching the tent and breaking camp.

To the beginner, a zipped-up tent offers inadequate security against attack from ill-intentioned persons or curious animals wandering on the camp site. For those who are worried about this aspect of camping, there is really no need for anxiety. Campers are usually friendly, cheerful people, and always ready to help should things go wrong.

City people are often apprehensive of the night noises on lonely farm sites and they are not used to the intense darkness and lack of traffic noise. However, after some days camping, they should get used to these conditions and feel secure in the tent at night.

The modern tent with sewn-in ground sheet and zipped entrance keeps out flying insects and creepy-crawlies. Providing the entrance *is* zipped-up, a light can be used at night and no moths or other insects can fly in to disturb the camper. With a sound ground sheet, water should not find its way into the tent. Modern plastic materials should allow the tent to lie in a puddle of water without any discomfort to the occupants.

Middle-aged persons who would like to camp tend to remember their military experiences 'under canvas'; the continual rain, the muddy slippery duckboards, wet equipment, too many men in one bell tent, and being bombarded with earwigs that clustered at the top of the tent pole.

Modern camping is *not* like that. In fact, a frame tent can be like a 'home from home' with every conceivable facility.

After the beginner has had some experience in general camping, he may like to consider backpacking. The backpacker is perhaps the elite one among campers, being well organised right down to the last half-ounce; nothing is left to chance but one should always bear in mind that if anything is going to go wrong, it will do!

Backpacking can be considered an Art, and like painting or

writing, a certain amount of thought must be devoted to the subject—particularly the equipment—before engaging in the activity. The backpacker must decide if cost is important, what items of the equipment will be home-made, and what is to be purchased. Catalogues must be scanned and each item considered and compared with similar ones offered in other catalogues. When looking at equipment in the shop, the judgement of the purchaser should not be swayed by advice from the assistant, who may know nothing about the problems of the backpacker. All items should be weighed before purchase, using a scale showing ounces/grammes, or better still fractions of ounces/grammes.

This little book offers some advice to the aspiring backpacker who wishes to *make* some of his own equipment at a considerable saving on shop prices.

The writer made his own tent because at the time there were no suitable tents available. Mostly they were too heavy, awkward to move around in, or too expensive. No information was available on making tents and by trial and error methods a prototype was constructed. This did not prove satisfactory and it was 'unpicked' and re-made into the 'distorted bell' later described in the book. In the writer's opinion it is a very satisfactory design for two persons, and perhaps a child up to ten years of age.

The prospect of making a tent, a sleeping bag or anorak may appear formidable at first, but reduced to logical progressive procedure it can be quite simple. No particular ability is needed, only common sense and a desire to achieve something; so that is the aim of this book, achievement and escape.

Those who have camped regularly for years, perhaps starting in their early youth with the Boy Scouts, Girl Guides or Youth organisations, may have to reconsider their equipment before trying backpacking. It is difficult to discard, say, a favourite rucksack, which may be too heavy. Lightness is all, providing a reasonable degree of comfort is available. My wife and I back-packed along some 112.63 km (70 miles) of Offa's Dyke in the summer of 1976. Between us—discounting the clothes we stood up in, the camera and lightweight telescope—we carried some 12.7 kg (28 lb). This was full camping equipment and included

3

1.8 kg (4 lb) of food. By further careful thought and planning, even this load could be reduced.

During this Offa's Dyke expedition, we met many young men backpacking, but oddly no women. It appeared to me that the prospect of carrying a heavy rucksack like the young men, did not appeal to them. Again, with careful planning, this activity of backpacking could be open to women as well as men. After all, many women trudge along with heavy shopping bags, far heavier than my wife's rucksack (which, incidentally, feels much lighter on the back than when carried in the hand).

One disadvantage of backpacking, is the difficulty in keeping clean. The backpacker is up early in the morning; the man shaves if he is unbearded, has a quick swill in his collapsible nylon bowl, and is ready for breakfast and away. This kind of toilet may not be sufficient for the fastidious woman, so that it would be either necessary to stop a day in three, say, for a good clean up, or have a bed and breakfast stop at a farm and obtain a bath there. This latter idea may not appeal to the backpacker purist, so that the only alternative could be a bath in a remote stream or mountain pool.

Those who have had general camping experience may find that they will have to modify their eating habits when backpacking. Food and cooking equipment can make a lot of weight in the rucksack. Adequate nourishment is necessary to maintain a good pace, but one can eat too much during the day. We find that a light breakfast first thing, with small amounts of food at regular intervals during the day, followed by a hot meal at night, are perfectly adequate to maintain our bodies in a healthy state. Glucose tablets are a useful addition to the daily diet.

The person who is worried about being overweight will soon start to slim after a week or ten days backpacking. Perhaps this is the answer for the overweight; plenty of rhythmic gentle exercise with a limited diet.

The backpacker must consider whether to walk alone or with one or more companions. The advantage of a companion or companions is that the load is shared, and the backpackers will carry less per person than the solo man on his own. Also, if one is

4

travelling alone, there is always the possibility of sickness or accident happening in some remote spot where help is not available.

The backpacker must also consider the aim in backpacking; is one out to break records, or does one wish to amble along for 20 km a day? If one wants to put in the mileage, any companions must be capable of keeping up and not be a drag. One must also choose compatible friends with similar habits. It is awkward, say, to arrange for one vegetarian among a party of non-vegetarians.

2
Making a Simple Tent

Perhaps the most important invention of this age for the back-packer and camper, has been *proofed nylon*. Lightweight, strong and waterproof, it would seem the ideal material for tents, anoraks and waterproof trousers. However, it does present a barrier to moisture both ways and so reduction of condensation is an important factor.

When designing a tent, one must make allowances for conden-sation and introduce some satisfactory method of ventilation. The writer has found that it is difficult to make a well-ventilated, single-skin tent—either the wind and rain are a problem, or the inside of the tent is running with condensation in the morning.

After considerable experiment—mainly of the trial and error kind—the writer came to the conclusion that the only practical way of avoiding condensation was by making an inner tent, and then a separate fly to cover it. Vapour from the sleeper rises through the roof of the inner tent, which is unproofed, and con-denses on the fly. Then any droplets of condensation fall on to the roof of the inner and not on the sleeper. If the fly is open at both ends, vapour can be carried away by a slight breeze.

In the morning, the fly is well shaken and soon dries out. This is a great advantage of nylon when compared with a cotton tent, which can take much longer to dry.

Dimensions

When the aspiring backpacker designs a solo tent, he must first of all consider his height, and add 76–100 mm (3–4 in) to it: this will be the length of the inner tent. If he is not a bulky man, the width should be about 760 mm (30 in). Then he must measure how tall he is sitting up; add 51 mm (2 in) and that will be the height of the tent. Such a tent drawn out on paper may seem perfectly satisfactory—until it is actually made up and tried, when any defects are apparent. Then the designer is faced with the trouble of dismantling and altering it. This difficulty can be avoided by careful planning.

Design

After deciding on the type of tent to be constructed, which we will assume is the usual two-pole ridge type, the linear outline of the inner is set up on the lawn, using garden canes and string as illustrated. The outline of the floor is pegged out first (Fig. 2.1(a)). Will it be large enough to accommodate the camper, his boots and spare kit, perhaps used as a pillow?

Two canes are pushed in the lawn at each centre end of the floor, string is stretched along the ridge and down each end and pegged to the floor (Fig. 2.1(b)). Guys are run off at each end of the ridge, to keep the canes upright (Fig. 2.1(c)), and all the string is checked to see that it is tight.

The designer must now try to get in and out of the tent lay-out by moving the tent pole to one side. The backpacker one-man tent is only for sleeping, so that ease in getting in and out is not too important. Is the designer sure there is sufficient headroom in which to sit and eat the evening meal? (Fig. 2.1(d)). Would there be more headroom if short walls were introduced to widen the headroom (Fig. 2.1(e))?

Satisfied by the size of the inner, the maker must then measure carefully the taut string and mark out on brown paper or wall-

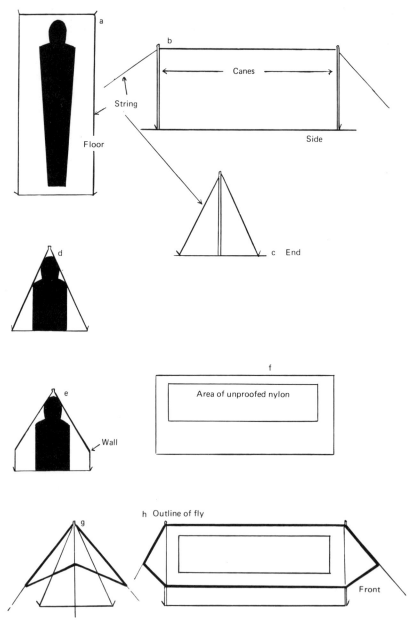

a

b

Canes

String

Floor

Side

c   End

d

e

Wall

f

Area of unproofed nylon

h   Outline of fly

g

Front

Fig. 2.1   Setting out the solo tent.

8

paper, patterns for the inner, not allowing for any seams. Patterns must also be made for proofed nylon margins round the edge of the roof and floor of the inner (Figs. 2.1(f) and 2.3(a)). If the designer is still anxious about the size of the tent, a prototype can be made up from the paper patterns fastened together with adhesive tape at the seams and erected on the lawn on a dry, windless day. The door patterns can be cut out as in Fig. 2.3(b), leaving a lip on the front edge of the floor. Provision must be made for inserting short lengths of tape for holding open the unzipped door.

The next task is to decide on the size of the fly. It should be large enough to project well over the sides of the tent and, preferably, a short hood should extend front and back along the guys. The entry end should have a larger hood to give protection during cooking.

Set up the canes again on the lawn and stretch string across to represent the fly, which should be about 76 mm (3 in) above the roof of the inner. Run the string across each end for the hoods and measure off and make patterns as before (Figs. 2.1(g) and (h)).

Material

We now have all the patterns ready and taking into account 20 mm (¾ in) approximately, seams, we can estimate how much proofed nylon will be needed. This material can be obtained in different weights per square yard, so it will be easy to decide what the weight of the tent will be to within an ounce or two.

The roof of the inner is made of unproofed nylon, often available from a market stall—it looks like a very fine net.

Having obtained samples and decided on the colour of the tent, on receipt of the proofed nylon, it should be rolled on a cardboard tube, or laid under the carpet to remove the creases. The material should not be ironed as the heat may affect it.

Lay out the patterns on the material allowing for the 20 mm (¾ in) seams and mark off. One can use a fine felt pen, though

9

this can make an indelible mark on the nylon. Cut out and keep the scraps as these will be useful at a later stage.

Sewing Techniques

Without proper facilities, sewing together sheets of proofed nylon can be a most frustrating business. Any sewing machine should be satisfactory and the maker can use an 'Atomloy Foot' (Fig. 2.2(a)) which consists of two small rollers which run smoothly across the surface of the material. A No. 11 ball-pointed needle should be used with a large reel of polyester thread of a suitable colour. Pin together long lengths of the scrap material, and setting the stitch at 8 or 10 to the inch, try machining long straight seams. Examine the stitch; is it loose one side? If so, adjust either the top or bottom tension or place a weight on the bobbin which may skid round during machining. Is the material puckered? The tension may be too tight, so adjust accordingly. Does the material crease? Adjust head pressure, or as a last resort pin and glue together with 'Copydex' before sewing up.

Fig. 2.2　Sewing machine and useful accessories; (a) 'Atomloy' foot, (b) ruffler.

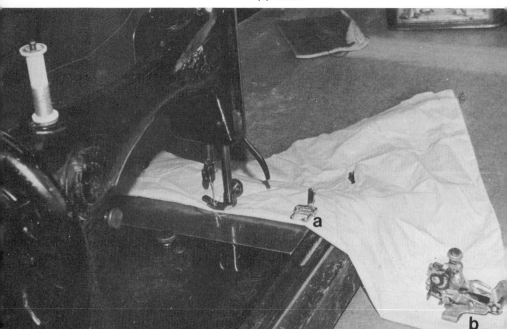

When the maker is confident that he can machine a neat seam, he can proceed with making up the tent. Handling large pieces of the slippery nylon is difficult and it is useful to have a large piece of hardboard on the table on which to support it. Let the material pass evenly under the foot with no pulling to one side. Check that pins do not become caught, so preventing the regular forward movement of the material.

Finish off the ends by knotting or using the reverse or darner on the sewing machine. It will be noticed that some seams are later oversewn by others, which helps to keep them from becoming undone.

Making the Inner Tent

Fold over long lengths of the proofed nylon scraps and machine down the centre, so that the strips are about 20 mm ($\frac{3}{4}$ in) wide. Cut into pieces about 76 mm (3 in) long and fold lengthways into a loop. These loops are inserted in the outer seams at the time of sewing (Fig. 2.3(a–c)) so that pegs or rubber bands can be tied to them to keep the tent rigid.

The most usual seam used in tent making is the run and fell. After the first seam has been sewn, 7 mm ($\frac{1}{4}$ in) is cut off one side of the seam and the other side turned over and under the cut off side, which is then sewn down so that the needle passes through four thicknesses (Fig. 2.3(c)). Before sewing the second seam, pin all the seam down firmly, putting in loops where necessary. Pass the seam slowly under the sewing machine, maintaining gentle tension to each side of the seam, and where necessary hold down by hand, so that the seam has a neat, flat finish. A little practice on scrap would be useful before attempting work on the seams. Where the roof of the inner is joined to the proofed nylon, turn one edge inside the other, as shown, to give a neat finish (Fig. 2.3(d)).

The material should be turned in both sides when putting the zips in at the front (Fig. 2.3(e)). Always use metal zips—plastic ones can burst open at the most inconvenient times. A 'zipper foot' attachment to the sewing machine is useful for inserting zips.

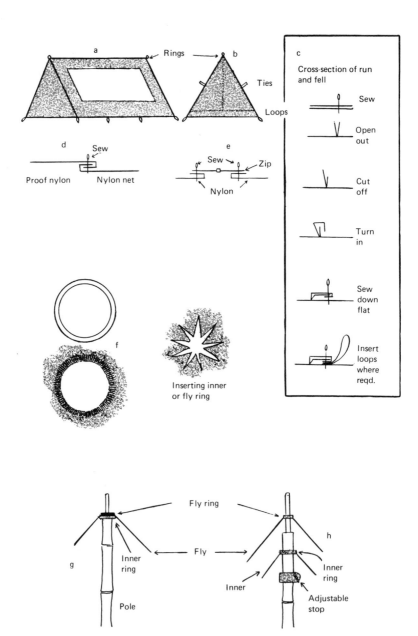

Fig. 2.3 Construction of the solo tent.

Making the Flysheet

The inner being more or less finished, suitable aluminium rings are sewn at each end of the ridge (Figs. 2.3(a) and (b)). The fly is then sewn up, using run and fell seams on ridge and hood ends. Where rings are inserted for the poles (Fig. 2.3(f)) cut small holes for rings—cut radially, turn over ring and hand sew over. The outer edges of the fly are turned in twice and the loops sewn in: rubber bands (sections of cycle inner tube) are pulled through the loops and lengths of lightweight nylon cord are attached as guys. The rubber bands make the guys self-tensioning. Lightweight alloy pegs can be purchased for the fly and bamboo ones made to hold down the inner floor.

Poles

Bamboo canes can be used for the tent poles and these, if made in two sections can be joined together with fishing rod ferrules or aluminium tube. Both ends should be tubed to slide inside each other, otherwise the poles may jam if wet. A little hole can be drilled at the base of the large tube to prevent suction. The base of each pole can be protected with a rubber walking-stick ferrule. The top of each pole has an insert of 7 mm ($\frac{1}{4}$ in) brass tubing set in with epoxy or polyester resin adhesive and bound or tubed round the outside to prevent splitting. The tubes pass through the rings in the fly and the poles stand outside the tent inner, so that the fly can be erected first in bad weather (Fig. 2.3(g)).

Floor

The floor seams should be adhesively taped to make them water-proof. If the floor is of very lightweight material, it is advisable to carry a thin polythene sheet to place underneath it. The seams should all be sprayed with a waterproofing agent and the tent is now ready.

3
Two Tent Designs for Two or Three Persons

Having made a solo tent, you may like to consider designing a larger one. Where two or more persons are involved, the important thing is the provision of adequate means of entrance and exit to the tent. Confusion can arise when the campers want to be either in or out of the tent at the same time and there is only one entrance.

Planning a 2–3 Person Tent

Probably the best kind of tent is the one with two separate entrances, so that the occupants can move in and out without too much difficulty.

Proceeding in the same way as when making the solo tent, the backpacker should lay out the floor area, and test the adequacy of the space with one or two friends. If the tent is to be ridge type or pyramid shape, will the sides of the tent interfere with movement when the campers are sitting up? Perhaps the wedge shape is better, as this allows room to sit up and the entrance can be from either upright side. Two poles on each upright side of the wedge and a ridge pole across provide a rigid structure for erecting the flysheet first when pitching the tent. The best position of the poles and ridge should then be determined by checking the arc of movement when the backpackers lie down and sit up, as it may be possible to have a tent of lower profile with the poles situated more towards the head end of the tent.

The inner tent is constructed in the usual way, with a proofed nylon tray for a groundsheet and a nylon net top; the upright sides can be of proofed nylon, with a ventilation panel if desired. One zip can be inserted parallel with the pole, and the other along the top of the groundsheet tray.

The fly must cover the ventilated parts of the inner adequately, and can extend to cover each upright side as a hood. When thinking about the design, one must decide where one is going to keep his spare kit, inside the tent, or outside under the fly, and plan the accommodation accordingly.

An Advanced Design

The distorted bell type of tent shown in Figs. 3.1–3.5 is more ambitious and has the advantage that only one pole is used, the ridge being maintained with two long guys. The entrance is more or less oblong and there is ease of entrance and exit. The size of the particular tent shown is suitable for two adults and perhaps a child of up to ten years of age. The head end is half-round and the campers sleep each side of the tent pole and the child below the pole, so that the nuisance of having a pole at the entrance is eliminated. There is some room at the back of the tent pole for storing items of kit. The floor tapers slightly towards the entrance and the walls are quite high to keep out the draught and wet, and are attached to the fly by hooks and rubber bands.

The top of the tent is in the shape of a long triangle (Fig. 3.3), the long guys holding it in tension. The base is over the entrance, the inner roof being attached to the fly with aluminium rings and hooks: this arrangement keeps the roof relatively rigid.

At the half-round end, the nylon net is supported with strips of proofed nylon turned in and sewn, to make a neat finish (Fig. 3.2). The top of the isosceles triangle of the roof and the nylon strip all meet at the large aluminium ring, through which the tent pole passes.

15

Fig. 3.1 'Inner' part of the two-person tent showing the entrance; (a) proofed nylon, (b) unproofed nylon

There is adequate room under the fly at each side in order to leave wet clothing. In severe weather, the lower section of the tent pole can be replaced with a shorter section and the fly pegged down directly to the ground, the inner being taken up inside and clipped together with clothes pegs. The tent then presents a low profile to any strong gales and there is less likelihood of it blowing away. The ventilation would be reduced of course, and there would be more condensation.

This tent and the G.R.P. (glass-reinforced plastic or fibreglass) frame described in Chapter 5 were made up together, the pole being of sufficient length when divided into two sections to form the arms of the frame. If backpackers are contemplating constructing this tent, they must bear this in mind when making their own. The top section of the pole has a length of tubing, just like the solo tent, pushed into the end and secured with G.R.P. to prevent any splitting. The tube passes through the small ring in the fly and the pole supports the fly. This inner is supported on a ring which rests on an adjustable metal collar, with a small bolt and fly nut securing it to the top section of the pole (Fig. 2.3(h)). The two sections are joined together using a suitable sized fishing

16

Fig. 3.2 'Head end of the inner part', (a) proofed nylon (b) unproofed nylon

Fig. 3.3 Side and entrance of the 'inner' part; (a) proofed nylon, (b) unproofed nylon.

Fig. 3.4   Entrance to fly sheet.

rod ferrule or aluminium tubing. The base of the pole is covered with a walking stick rubber ferrule.

Having set out the floor using pegs and string, erect the pole and lay out the inner tent. This design is far more complicated than the others and great care must be taken to ensure that the measurements are correct. When satisfied, proceed with the construction of the inner and when it is finished, set it up on the lawn and proceed to make the fly. The fly must be larger than the inner, of course, to allow for a suitable air space to carry away the condensation. The distance between the rings at the top, between fly and inner, should be about 102 mm (4 in). The long isosceles triangle of the inner top (which can be made of proofed nylon) should be clipped closely to the fly with rings and hooks, to make a rigid structure. The nylon net will hang from the edge of the inner roof and the fly should be arranged to veer away from it.

When camping, it may be found that the site will not allow the long guys to be extended. If this is not practical, the entrance can be propped up with sticks (Fig. 3.4).

Fig. 3.5 Head end of fly sheet.

The fly can be erected first (Figs. 3.4 and 3.5); the pole is then removed and pushed through the ring of the inner, which is erected under cover of the fly.

4
Making a Sleeping Bag

As with a tent, the dimensions of the sleeping bag depend on the size of the person using it. It should not be necessary to have a long sleeping bag when the user is short, as the excess length is only more bulk and weight to carry. It should, however, be long enough to cover the head on cold nights and to allow one to curl up. The tapered kind of sleeping bag is probably the most satisfactory, the shape of the bag fits it close to the nether portions of the body, while the oblong kind of bag can have cold spots at the feet when the sleeper shifts about in the night.

It is very important that the width at the top around the trunk is sufficient for movement. I find it ideal to allow 508 mm (20 in) for free movement over and above my chest measurement. A bulky person would perhaps require more room than one of average weight.

Should the sleeping bag have a zip on or is the closed type the best? Zips can go wrong; they can jam or break, usually at inconvenient times, and the backpacker is faced with a miserable night trying to keep the gap closed. If a zip is wanted in the sleeping bag, it should be backed by a long 'bar' of nylon tubing stuffed with down to prevent the cold air coming in through the chinks in the zip runner. Many prefer the closed 'mummy' type sleeping bag without the zip. After a little practice it is easy enough to wriggle into the bag without much effort, the draw string at the top keeps the bag closely round the neck and keeps in the heat and the draught out. It is not often at night that it feels too hot for comfort, and if it is, the draw string is loosened, and the sleeper soon cools off.

At the present time, perhaps the best material to use for making a sleeping bag is downproof nylon. This material allows the body to breathe, as the water vapour given off by the sleeper during the night passes through the material. Some people do not like the smooth feel of nylon against them and prefer downproof cambric, which can be purchased quite easily. The inner part can be sewn up using downproof cambric, the outer being made of the nylon. Those striving for extra lightness could use all-nylon instead, as the cambric is quite heavy material compared with the nylon.

Several different kinds of fillings are available for the bag; goose down, duck down, and down and feather. The beginner may not like to take a chance with using new filling and may have an old eiderdown available. The disadvantage of using old eiderdowns is that the contents have perhaps been compressed over the years and the down (or down and feathers) has lost the capacity to 'plump up' the sleeping bag and maintain good insulation. One great disadvantage with down (or down and feather) filling is the fact that the filling compresses when the backpacker lies upon it; cold spots can be felt through the floor of the tent at the hips, knees or shoulders, so an air bed or a plastic foam mat should be used for sleeping on.

When the sleeping bag is constructed, the down is contained in channels, each channel being separate and sealed, so that the down cannot 'creep' out of one channel into another. It is very important that no outlet remains between channels or the 'creeping' down may leave a cold spot, and the maker will be obliged to dismantle his bag to rectify the fault.

Perhaps the most efficient kind of bag has narrow channels across the bag rather than lengthways. A shaped foot at the bottom can allow ease of movement at the bottom of the bag (Fig. 4.1(c)).

Patterns can be made up of strong paper and a prototype inner bag constructed, then the backpacker must wriggle into it to see if

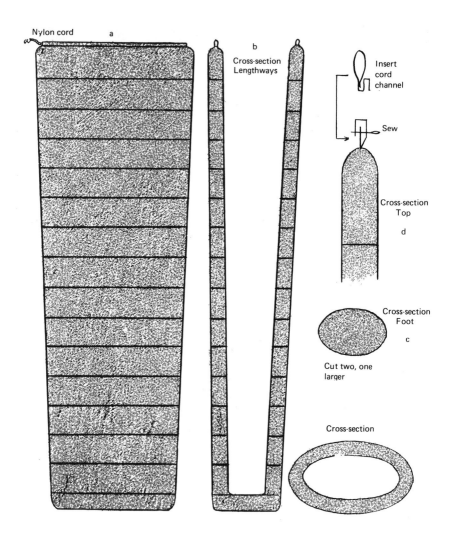

Nylon cord

a

b
Cross-section
Lengthways

Insert
cord
channel

Sew

Cross-section
Top

d

Cross-section
Foot

c

Cut two, one
larger

Cross-section

Fig. 4.1   Making up the sleeping bag.

there is sufficient width to allow movement when turning over. The inner is then cut out and made up and the outer cover is constructed. This is, of course, of greater diameter than the inner, to allow room for the down, and the two are joined together by the channels, and at the top, and foot. One side seam on the outer cover is left open for the down to be inserted into the channels and the side seam is then sewn up and the draw cord inserted at the top.

Fig. 4.1(a) shows a suitable 'mummy' type sleeping bag which can be altered to suit the maker's particular dimensions as required. A zip can be used with this bag if desired. Measure carefully the amount of material required. Lay it out on the floor and mark out with tailors chalk (which can be erased) or a fibre pen (which could make an indelible mark) the shape of the inner and the position of the channels, and cut out—allowing for seams as when making the tent.

Sew the inner bag together first, inserting the foot and using a run and fell seam, but leaving one side seam open. The channel sides are made of nylon jersey, available from the market stall, cut into strips 63 mm (2½ in) wide; this allows for 13 mm (½ in) seams each side.

Before starting to sew, the machine should be set for eight to ten stitches to the inch. Also, the tension should be adjusted, using scraps of material until the stitch tension is satisfactory and there is no crimping of the material. A No. 11 ball-pointed needle can be used, either with nylon or downproof cambric. Sew the channel edges to the marked lines on the inner, allowing a 25 mm (1 in) margin at each end where the channels meet the open side seam. The use of the 'Ruffler' attachment (Fig. 2.2) on the sewing machine is invaluable for doing this because the outer edge of the channel has to be the same length as the marked positions on the outer cover, while the inner edge of the channel has to be accommodated to a shorter distance on the inner cover (Fig. 4.1(b). Some initial experiment with the 'Ruffler' is advised to determine the tension of the two materials used. After practicing on odd bits of material, the inner edge of the first channel should be pinned at intervals to the marked position on the inner, allowing for loose material on the channel in between the pins. Using the 'Ruffler', the loose material should be accommodated between the pins so that the channels are sewn evenly all round the inner.

The outer cover is now cut out, remembering that it is wider than the inner, to allow for the down filling. The writer's sleeping bag outer was 127 mm (5 in) wider overall than the inner, allowing for 13 mm ($\frac{1}{2}$ in) seams. The channel positions are marked off in the same way and the outer channel edges are joined to the outer cover. The top is sewn together, run and fell, inserting an open-ended channel to take the draw cord as shown in Fig. 4.1(d). Leave a gap in the foot to insert the down. The open inner side seam is now sewn using a run and fell seam, and it may be necessary to loosen off the channel seams to accomplish this. The channel ends are fastened to one another, using hand stitching and 'Copydex' adhesive. At these points make sure that there are no spaces where the down can escape. The bag is now ready to receive the filling.

Some people are allergic to down and they should wear some kind of mask or respirator when handling it. The work-place must be specially prepared. A bathroom or caravan are ideal places to stuff the bag. Move out all carpets so that the workplace is as bare as possible. Curtains should be taken down and draughts eliminated. Down is an elusive kind of substance and can drift into all kinds of places; and it is very difficult to clear up afterwards. If possible the sleeping bag should be supported on a broomstick so that the mouths of the channels are facing upwards. The end of the stick can be clamped in a vice or it can be rested across the ends of a bath.

If the maker intends to dismantle an eiderdown, this can best be done by using a large plastic bag, the type in which mattresses are supplied. Weigh the bag; if there are any holes, fasten them up with sellotape to prevent the down from puffing out. Place the eiderdown in the plastic bag, insert the hands and with scissors, slash open the eiderdown at the far end. Gently tease out the down and when a channel is clear, cut off that piece of cover material and withdraw it from the plastic bag. Careful and deliberate movements are essential to prevent the down flying about. Continue this procedure until the plastic bag is full of down and the remnants of the eiderdown cover have been withdrawn. Weigh the bag to find the weight of the down.

Warmth in the sleeping bag at night is essential and the backpacker must make sure that his bag will be warm enough. The writer used an old eiderdown to make his bag and it was not warm enough at first. The total weight was then 1.4 kg (3 lb) so he added another 0.2268 kg (half pound) of down and feather and the heat retention was improved. The cover, empty, weighed about 0.5 kg (1 lb), so that the maker could expect to use about 1.1340 kg (2½ lb) of old eiderdown stuffing for his bag.

The total cubic capacity of the channels must then be determined and the down filling divided accordingly among the channels. An accurate weighing device is essential. An old coin balance is useful, with slips of thin metal as weights—say 5 g or ¼ oz. Half a dozen plastic bags, all weighing the same, are used to insert the down into the channels.

The bags should be long and sleeve-like. The openings should be rolled back on themselves and when filled with down, the open ends turned over and clipped with a clothes peg until the down can be inserted in the channels.

When inserting the down, hold the opening of the bag firmly closed with one hand, remove the peg, and push the end of the bag into the channel, easing it inside out with the aid of the turned back portion. Push the bottom of the plastic bag into the channel so that the down is well inside, then withdraw the bag (turned inside out) from the channel, the end of which is turned over and closed with the clothes peg. Continue the procedure until the channels are all filled. Gently remove all the pegs and pin the outer side edges of the bag together after coating the inner surfaces and parts of adjoining channels with 'Copydex'. When dry, the seam is sewn up, turned in on itself and sewn again. A nylon cord of sufficient length is then inserted through the top of the bag and tied so that it cannot creep out. Shake the bag well, turning it round and round to distribute the down evenly.

Those who require a zipper down the side will have to leave the inner and outer side seams open until the bag is stuffed; the ends of the channels are then sewn over and the zip inserted *inside the bag* in the way described in making up the tent. A bar of nylon with down filling should be sewn in with the zip inside the bag. This prevents draughts and reduces heat loss considerably.

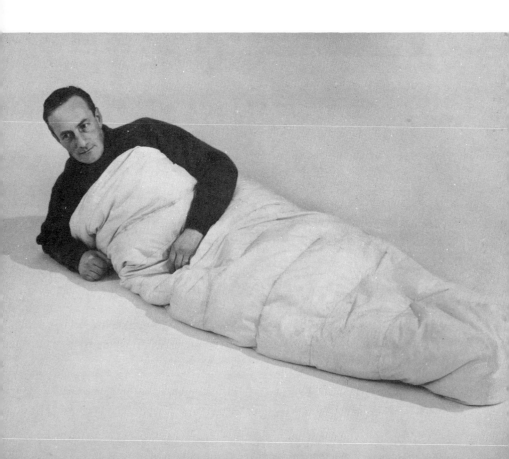

5

Making a Combined Tent Pole and Carrying Frame

Many backpackers prefer to carry a frame with their rucksack. The frame holds the load rigid and there is a space between the back surface of the rucksack and the back of the walker to allow the perspiration to escape. Wearing a frame prevents the walker's back being soaked with sweat and consequent chilling, when the load is removed during a rest period or setting up camp.

The frame can be a cumbersome article in a small tent, especially when the rucksack is attached to it. To overcome this difficulty, a collapsible frame was built up consisting of a sub-frame and of the tent pole divided into two sections (Fig. 5.1). The advantages of this frame are that it is light, it can be dismantled quickly and the sub-frame wrapped up with the carrying straps takes up very little room. The solo walker (carrying a conventional rucksack or the 'cricket bag' type of rucksack described in Chapter 8), or the backpacker in a party (carrying the sleeping bags or tents, rolled up as in Fig. 5.3) could find this frame a most useful piece of equipment.

The two-section tent pole is made of bamboo garden cane, and has already been described in Chapter 3. However, the maker may instead prefer to buy two sections of G.R.P. fishing rod. It is possible to make a G.R.P. pole oneself, but the writer has found that it is not worth the trouble. It was difficult to form the rods satisfactorily, and weight-for-weight they were not as substantial as bamboo.

The sub-frame is constructed of G.R.P. (glass-reinforced plastic or glassfibre). The backband is either wide nylon tape or deck-chair canvas; the supporting straps can be of webbing (car safety belts are useful) or leather straps off an old rucksack.

Like most of the other equipment, the size of the frame depends on the size of the wearer. Perhaps about 635 mm (25 in) is about right for the average person. It is important not to make the frame too high, as the top can catch in projecting tree branches when the walker is ducking his head underneath. Likewise, the bottom portion can catch on gates when the walker is scrambling over them. If in doubt, the maker should construct the sub-frame first and fit garden canes to find the most convenient size for the frame/tent poles. The supports of the sub-frame waist band should not press against the body, so that allowance must be made for this if the backpacker is wide across the hips.

Fabricating the sub-frame is quite a simple job, providing everything is arranged beforehand. Glass reinforced plastic is a strong material and is quite adequate for making the sub-frame— though, of course, anyone who can work in aluminium may prefer to make the sub-frame of that metal.

It will be seen from the illustrations that the sub-frame consists of a transverse oval tube, with short tubes at an angle each end to take the two parts of the tent pole. The base extends to form a waist band support. It is necessary to make up an oval tube 32 × 20 mm (1¼ × ¾ in) and 241 mm (9½ in) long or more to suit; cover this with the glassfibre mat soaked in resin.

One end of each half of the tent pole has a strip of greased paper wrapped round it and the glassfibre mat and resin is rolled round to form the two end sockets. When the G.R.P. is set hard, the canes can be pulled out and the paper scraped out of the sockets—so that the canes can be pushed in and out easily. The side pieces and top of the sub-frame are cut out of glassfibre sheet and all the pieces are fabricated together with glassfibre mat and resin. Finally, the waist belt is rivetted to the frame and the straps buckled on. It is now ready for use.

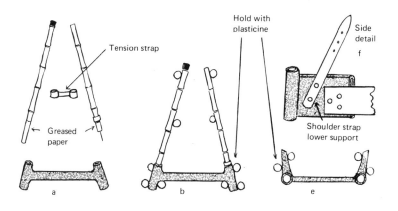

Hold with plasticine

Tension strap

Greased paper

Side detail

f

Shoulder strap lower support

a

b

e

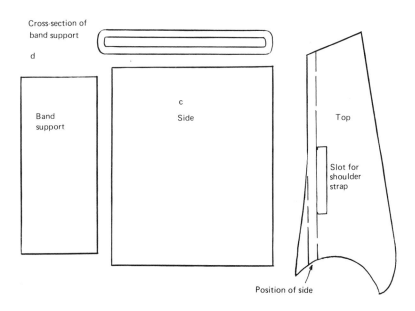

Cross-section of band support

d

Band support

c

Side

Top

Slot for shoulder strap

Position of side

Fig. 5.1 Construction details of the carrying frame.

29

Using G.R.P.

Glassfibre work is best carried out in a well-ventilated workshop. The resin has a strong smell which can be irritating to the throat and chest and a suitable mask or respirator should be worn. The smell tends to linger even when the G.R.P. articles and equipment are removed from the workshop, so it is not advisable to do this work in the house. The best place is probably a garage with the doors open. The resin, which looks remarkably like honey, is usually supplied in a tin, together with a liquid or paste hardener. A small percentage of hardener is added to the resin, which solidifies in about half an hour at 16°C (60°F). Glassfibre mat is wetted with the resin and hardener, which forms a strong material when set.

Make up the oval transverse tube out of thin cardboard and push a piece of stick through so that the ends project. Rest the ends of the stick over a box, or put one end of the stick in a vice so that both hands can be used. Wearing gloves, cut out with sharp scissors a piece of glassfibre mat (300 gm material) sufficient to roll round the oval tube *three* times. Mix up sufficient resin and hardener to wet the mat. The resin is very sticky and difficult to remove from the hands, so polythene gloves should be worn, or a barrier cream used on the hands. (*It is important to observe the maker's safety precautions when handling any of these materials:* avoid inhaling vapour, skin or eye contact, or ingestion. The worker should not smoke and the materials should be kept away from a naked flame).

With a stiff brush, wet the oval tube with resin all over and hold the edge of the glassfibre mat against it. Stipple the mat with the resin-loaded brush, until the mat becomes malleable. Turn the tube gradually, stipple the mat until soft and slowly roll the cardboard tube in the softened glassfibre mat three times. Make sure that it is all wetted out and there are no air bubbles. Bubbles can be avoided by evenly rolling the mat on the tube. Place the tube on one side to set and wash the brush in a cleaning solution.

Take the tent pole and roll greased paper round the ferrule

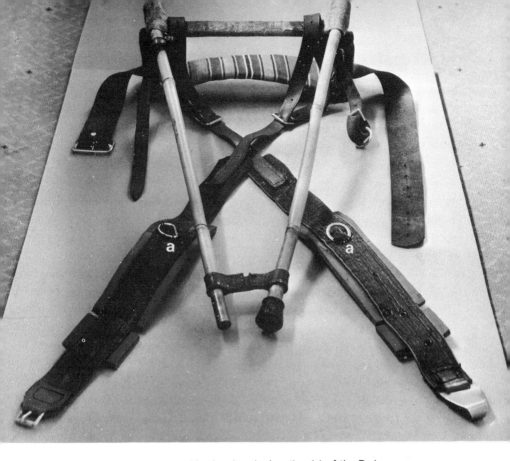

Fig. 5.2 Frame assembly showing the location (a) of the D-rings.

end of the bottom section. Greased paper should be rolled round the top (spike end) of the other section and the spike should be greased (Fig. 5.1(a)). Lay the mat upon the pole, using the same method treatment as for the oval tube, and set aside to harden. When the parts have hardened, push the stick out of the oval tube and using a rasp, roughen the glassfibre ends and the tentpole sockets where they will join together. Cut some glassfibre mat into short lengths of about 13 mm ($\frac{1}{2}$ in) and tease them apart. Mix a small amount of resin and hardener and rub in the glass-fibre strands until the resin forms a stiff, glutinous mass which will not run. Place a newspaper on the floor or table, and lay out upon it the two tent poles with sockets and the oval tube. Using plasticine to hold the parts in place, arrange the poles and oval tube in the correct relative positions, as shown (Fig. 5.1(b)). The angle from the vertical should be about 10°. Fill the gaps round the sockets and oval tube with the glassfibre and resin mix and leave it to harden.

Fig. 5.3   The frame complete with load.

Make a template of the side and top supports illustrated in Fig. 5.1(c), enlarged to suit the sockets. A pair of each will be required, one set for each side of the frame. Lay the patterns on a piece of glass and arrange them so that the pieces are as close together as possible. Mark the area on the glass with a fibre pen or wax pencil, remove the paper patterns and grease the marked area. Cut three pieces of glass-fibre mat to fit the marked area; mix sufficient resin and place the first piece of mat on the marked area. 'Wet' it thoroughly with resin and add the second piece of mat. 'Wet' this in the same way and then repeat with the third piece, making sure there are no bubbles. Leave to set, trace the patterns on to the G.R.P. and then peel it off the glass. The shapes can be cut out with a fretsaw, or failing that, a hacksaw, finishing off with the rasp. The band supports (Fig. 5.1(d)) are moulded on thick cardboard to match the side pieces.

The parts that are to be joined together must be thoroughly roughened up with the rasp and then joined using the resin and glassfibre strand mix as before (Fig. 5.1(e). Leave the made-up frame for a week to fully cure and then check it for strength, reinforced where necessary.

If required, the sub-frame can be painted with powder colour (available from an art shop), mixed with resin and hardener to a suitable consistency. Before painting, rub the frame over with wire wool to provide a good 'key' for the paint.

The waistband is made of strong nylon tape or deckchair material, wide enough to fit the band supports, plus 13 mm ($\frac{1}{2}$ in) seams and 457 mm (18 in) long. Fold lengthways, sew down one side, leaving a 13 mm ($\frac{1}{2}$ in) margin. Turn it inside out and sew up again, using buttonhole thread with a large needle in the sewing machine, and a medium stitch. Pull the band through the band supports, turn in on itself, and sew by hand. If desired, a section of foam plastic or rubber can be inserted in the waistband for more comfort.

The waist belt can either be made of wide nylon tape or leather and is attached to the sub-frame with copper splay-out rivets, the kind used for leather work (Fig. 5.1(f)). Bore three holes for the rivets on each side of the sub-frame. Punch or cut corresponding

33

Fig. 5.4   Carrying position of the completed frame.

holes in the ends of the belt, push the rivets through the belt and frame, open out, and secure with the resin/glassfibre/strand mix, and sew on buckle.

In the same way attach the shoulder support lower straps to the sub-frame (Fig. 5.1 (f)). The right-hand lower strap is perforated at regular intervals of, say, 25 mm or 1 in to allow for adjustment. The left-hand strap has a buckle and ring as shown in Fig. 5.2. This also has perforations for adjustment.

The adjustable shoulder cross straps are fitted to the oval tube as shown (Fig. 5.2) and retained in place with a short strip of stainless steel on each side. Drill each end of the strips, place in position, drill the glassfibre sub-frame and fix with self-tapping screws set in resin.

The right-hand upper strap has a buckle for adjustment and the left-hand strap has a hook fabricated from sheet stainless steel (Fig. 5.2). Cut out the hook with shears, bend over in the vice, drill out the slot and finish with the file so that there are no sharp spots. Push the strap through the slot and hand sew with strong cobbler's thread.

Sew two D-rings to the shoulder straps where shown in Fig. 5.2. These rings take the load-retaining cord and hold the rucksack on roll of bedding close to the back of the neck to maintain a good balance.

Finally, a strap is made up to hold the top ends of the tent pole section together under tension (Fig. 5.1 (a)), sufficient room being left round one of them to enable it to be withdrawn.

6

Making a Showerproof Coat

The backpacker who has made the tent and sleeping bag should find no difficulty in making this useful, showerproof coat. The shoulders are reinforced with leathercloth to take the pull of the rucksack straps and to help protect the wearer from the unexpected downpour. The sleeves terminate in leathercloth cuffs around the wrists. These cuffs should not become soggy with the rain running down the sleeves and they also help to prevent the sleeve being pushed up when climbing through hedges; the elasticated leathercloth belt keeps the coat close to the waist, retaining the heat. This can be unbuckled and the coat unzipped in warm weather. The two zippered, flapped pockets at the front are useful to keep valuables in and they also can be made the correct size to take Ordnance Survey Maps. Whether or not to have pockets at the bottom of the coat is a matter of choice, as they can easily become filled with water during a storm and leave the contents soaking wet. The possibility of this happening can be reduced by fitting zippers and flaps to the pockets.

Material

The material for making this could be showerproof poplin or gabardine. This material can often be purchased from a market. The front zip fastener should be a substantial metal one, with both ends open. If one wishes, the inner side of the pocket flaps and the inner facing can be made of a contrasting material such as tartan, to give a touch of colour to the garment.

Pattern and Fit

A good fit is essential for this coat so it is impractical to give diagrams in this book from which enlarged patterns could be made; there would be some loss of accuracy during that process.

The maker is recommended to find a pattern for his or her particular size and adapt this to suit the design of this coat. The pattern to look for is an unlined jacket with a zipped front and set-in sleeve, preferably the battledress blouse type, with a deep collar. The blouse should be extended to coat length by sticking paper on to the body patterns and extending the seams straight down without tapering the waist; the front facings too are extended likewise. Allow a generous turn-up for the hem. Ignore any instructions about elasticating the waist or cuffs. A trouser pattern may be included with the blouse pattern which would be useful for making up the waterproof trousers described in Chapter 7.

Making the Coat

Full directions are usually included with the pattern and these should be followed when making up the coat. More material will be required than stated in the instructions. Before buying, visit a market stall or store and find out the widths of cloth available. The patterns should be laid out on the floor and the amount of cloth required ascertained. Always err on the generous side; it is better to have too much cloth than not enough.

Make up the garment as far as possible, with the exception of adding the cuffs, shoulder reinforcement, pockets and belt. It is important to be very accurate when making up the pockets in order to give them a neat appearance. Also, they must be carefully aligned in relation to the shoulder, side and centre seams.

37

It is advisable to make up a trial pocket from scraps of material—as an experiment—before working the actual coat pockets. The general principle of making a pocket is that it is constructed on the outside of the coat then pulled through the opening into the inside and finished, presenting a neat appearance on the outside. Each pocket consists of a flap, which is constructed of two pieces of material and a piece of interfacing; two welts and a zip for the pocket opening, plus two pocket sections for making the actual inner pocket.

As mentioned before, the inner material of the flap can be of some contrasting material. Preferably, the flap should be slightly wider than the pocket opening, to cover it against rain and present a neat appearance.

Mark the pocket position on the coat with chalk as shown (Fig. 6.1(a)), 25 × 152 mm (1 × 6 in); make a paper pattern for the flap allowing 20 mm (¾ in) seams, and cut out four in material and two in interfacing. Bear in mind the right and wrong sides of the material, which should be perfectly flat without creases or wrinkles.

To make a pocket flap, baste two pieces of material with right sides together; make sure that the pieces lie together well and baste on the interfacing; sew round the seam with normal stitch, fastening ends and leaving the top edge unsewn. Cut out the basting stitches; cut off bottom corners—not too near the seams (Fig. 6.1(f))—and turn inside out, pushing out the corners gently to get the correct shape. Press the flap, easing it over the outer material so that the seams do not show.

Cut out four pieces of material, each 203 mm (8 in) long by 51 mm (2 in) wide. These pieces are folded lengthways down the middle, wrong sides together, and are called welts (Fig. 6.1(b)). Press and place on pocket position with folded edges outside, open edges together (Fig. 6.1(c)). The pocket flap (Fig. 6.1(d)) must be inserted under the top welt as shown, and the top edge of the flap trimmed if necessary (Fig. 6.1(e)). The ends of the welts should extend equally on each side beyond the pocket position. Stitch

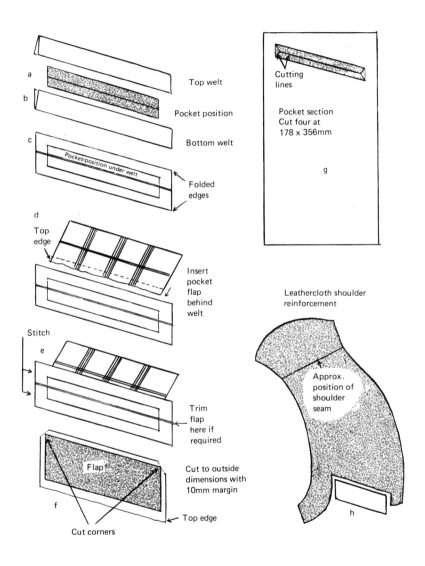

a

Top welt

Cutting
lines

b

Pocket position

Pocket section
Cut four at
178 x 356mm

c

Bottom welt

Pocket position under welt

Folded
edges

g

d

Top
edge

Insert
pocket
flap
behind
welt

Leathercloth shoulder
reinforcement

Stitch

e

Trim
flap
here if
required

Approx.
position of
shoulder
seam

Flap

Cut to outside
dimensions with
10mm margin

f

Top edge

h

Cut corners

Fig. 6.1   Details for making coat pocket and shoulder.

39

along the centre lines of each welt, which should coincide with the marked lines of the pocket position (Fig. 6.1(e)). Secure the ends of the thread. Pin one pocket section (Fig. 6.1(g)) in place on top of welt and flap, baste in place and machine along the stitching lines again. Cut through pocket layer and coat material between the open edges of the welts to within about 20 mm (three quarters of an inch) of the ends, and then diagonally into the corners as shown (Fig. 6.1(g)) as near to the stitching as possible without cutting it.

Turn the pocket into the inside of the coat, pulling in the V-shaped corners and the projecting ends of the welts through the cut material. The lips of the welts should meet without there being a gap or overlapping. The material should be manipulated and hand basted until the pocket looks neat. The ends of the pocket can be finished by bar tacking on the machine, or by hand stitching, after stitching the V-shapes in place.

The zip is now inserted between the lips of the welts, and sewn into place. On the inside, the second pocket section is pinned over the first and sewn round, leaving a margin of about 25 mm (1 in). Do *not* sew through the coat material. Sew again round the pocket between the seam and outer edge to make secure. Tack the front facing to the pocket seam, loosely, by hand.

Cuffs

Make up the cuffs—a pattern of thin card should be used. They should just be large enough to slip over the hands. Turn in the edges all round and stick down with, say, 'Copydex'. The inside can be lined if required; turn in the edges of the lining and sew round bottom edge with the machine, using a leather stitching needle and a long stitch with button-hole thread. It may be necessary to adjust the pressure of the foot and the tension when stitching leathercloth. To attach the cuffs, run a tacking thread round the sleeves and pull until the sleeve will fit into the cuff. Turn the cuff inside out (Fig. 6.3), insert the sleeve into the

Fig. 6.2   Front of the finished coat, showing pockets and belt.

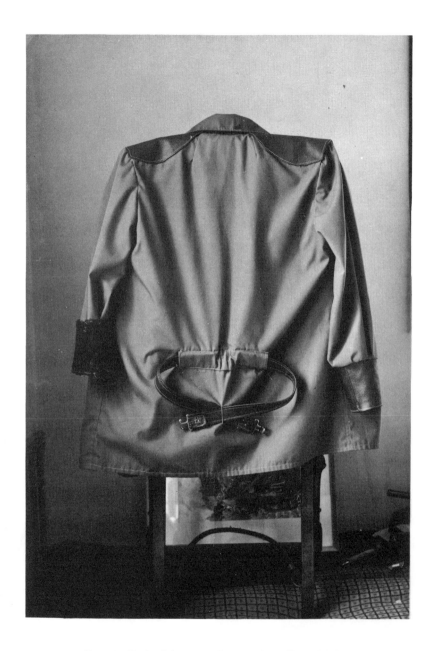

Fig. 6.3   Back of the coat, showing the cuffs and belt.

narrow end of the cuff, ease round and sew the sleeve round the top of the cuff under lining. Turn the cuff back again.

Shoulders

Cut out leathercloth to fit the shoulders to shape shown in Figs. 6.1(h) and 6.2, checking that it will fit the coat turn in, and stick down edges with 'Copydex'. Two shoulder pieces will be required and are stitched to the coat in the same manner as the cuffs. If a yoke is required across the back, the leathercloth must be cut into three parts to follow the shoulder seams of the coat, and joined there.

Belt

The belt is made of a 76 mm (3 in) strip of leathercloth of suitable length (Fig. 6.2). Turn in the edges and stick down; fold down the middle and sew round. The buckles can be attached with copper leather work rivets. Cut the belt in half at the back and sew the cut ends to a strip of strong elastic so that the belt will stretch to suit the figure. The elastic is hidden at the back by a panel of material sewn on as shown (Fig. 6.3). Turn in the edges of the panel before attaching to the garment and sew the elastic to the coat under the panel, so that the belt will not become lost.

7
Other Clothing

The backpacker must choose clothes to suit his own particular needs. Some people feel the cold more than others and will require more clothing than those who become overheated with walking.

Probably the best kind of clothing for walking consists of a string or cellular vest, cotton shirt and pants, one or two woollen jumpers, shorts or trousers. This kind of outfit allows the perspiration to escape and can help to prevent the body becoming overheated or chilled. Paper disposable pants are not much use as they soon disintegrate due to the action of walking.

Shorts or Trousers?

Shorts are a matter of choice. They allow more freedom, and legs that get wet with the rain soon dry again; on the other hand, the legs are exposed to nettles, brambles and barbed wire and can be badly scratched. The backpacker could wear shorts and pull on his waterproof nylon overtrousers should he feel chilled.

Boots

Boots, too are a matter of choice. They should not be too small, as the feet can tend to swell when they get hot. The condition of the feet is very important to the backpacker and correctly fitting boots are a 'must'. Two pairs of socks can be worn in the boots, or some people prefer a thin pair next to the feet and a thick, woollen pair on top. When walking long distances it is advisable to rub the inside of the inner pair of socks with wet soap, as this can be more comfortable for the feet. Gaiters are useful to wear with the boots as they prevent soiling of the lower parts of the trousers and help to prevent water seeping into the tops of the boots. Proper walking boots are the most suitable as Army-type boots can be heavy and cause discomfort.

Waterproof Clothing

With nylon waterproof outer clothing there is the same problem of condensation that we have with the tents. Some walkers have no trouble with nylon trousers and anoraks, but many discover that they are very wet after a day's walking, and think that their anorak is letting in the rain—when they are actually wet with perspiration.

One way of solving this problem is to wear a cycle cape with plastic sou'wester (Fig. 7.2). With this gear the backpacker could survive the heaviest thunderstorm without getting wet. Unfortunately, the cycle cape is not designed to accommodate a large pack, and in addition it tends to blow up over the backpacker's head in mountainous windy districts.

Before starting to make clothing, the backpacker must consider carefully if it is worth while. At the time of writing, some anoraks and waterproof trousers in nylon can be purchased for little more than the cost of material: the anorak particularly is awkward to make but waterproof trousers are quite simple.

Overtrousers

Measure round the hips, allowing for clothing and ease of movement, making sure there is room to pull the trousers over the boots,

45

and adjust pattern to suit. The waist measurement to be the same as the hip measurement. Sew up the inner and outer seams of the trousers using a run and fell seam; turn in the bottom of the trousers and sew. Insert elastic at the top in a turned in seam and the overtrousers are ready.

Anorak

If the backpacker intends to make an anorak the patterns for the showerproof coat can be used. If the anorak is to fit over the showerproof coat, it must be slightly larger to allow ease of movement. Pockets can be inserted if required, but they can fill with water in a heavy downpour.

Instead of the collar on the showerproof coat, a hood can be made for the anorak (Fig. 7.1). The neck edge should suit the neck edge of the anorak so that it is easier to sew in. Turn in the front edge of the hood and insert a cord knotted at each end to pull the hood close to the face. A cord too can be put in the bottom seam to keep the garment close if required.

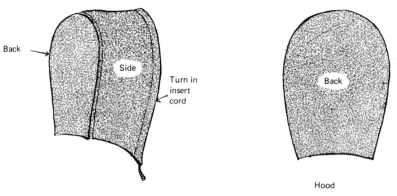

Back

Side

Turn in
insert
cord

Back

Hood

Fig. 7.1 Details of the hood.

46

A long flap can be sewn down the front of the anorak to cover the zip; this will prevent rain driving in through the zip. The flap should be held down at intervals with heavy press studs. Back up the studs with small pieces of nylon tape, to prevent too much pull on the proofed nylon and sew through.

Waterproof garments can be finished off by spraying the seams with a waterproofing agent, or sealing them with adhesive tape.

If uncertain as to the fit of the anorak, make it up first out of an old bed sheet to test the fit. Some walkers find an attached hood can cause headaches or a stiff neck, so sufferers could have the collar retained with a separate hood.

Shorts

Shorts with pockets and a fly are complicated to make and are not really worth the trouble. However, the backpacker who is interested in a pair of boxer-type shorts with elasticated waist can easily make them up by adapting the trouser pattern to his particular measurements. A showerproof gaberdine or poplin would be useful materials to make this garment. A market is probably the best source, where often remnants can be picked up cheaply.

Hats and Gloves

Those who knit can purchase wool and patterns and make up their woolly hats and gloves to their own colour scheme.

Cape

Probably the most useful waterproof garment is the cape which can reduce the problem of condensation. One great disadvantage of anoraks and cagouls is that when the rain stops, the backpacker has to remove his load in order to take off his anorak or cagoul.

Fig. 7.2   The cape as worn, with sou'wester.

The advantage of the cape is that the backpacker can roll it up at the front and push it back over his load where it is ready for instant use should it rain again. The bottom of the cape can be tied below the rucksack or load to prevent it falling off, and serves to protect it from the rain. An adapted cape is particularly useful with the zipped 'cricket-bag' type of rucksack as it can prevent water entering the zip fastener.

Some cycle capes are provided with thumb holds under the cape. These, together with the back fastening, can help to prevent the cape flying up with the wind.

The size and shape of the rucksack and load will vary from person to person, so that the back of the cape must be adapted to fit over the owner's particular load. Seams used throughout are the usual run and fell, and if possible, all the seams should be taped to prevent the entry of water. The hood pattern for the anorak can be used for the cape as a separate item, or a sou'wester purchased.

Many cycle capes are made of plastic which tears easily when sewn, so that it is advisable to seek the manufacturer's advice on how to insert additional panels into this kind of material.

A small towel can often be used with advantage in wet weather. Wrapped round the neck it prevents the odd trickle finding its way down the collar. Insert a nylon tie with hook and ring to hold the cape on the rucksack or load: an alternative is to make a tube of nylon with elastic inside under tension to keep the cape in place. Cut a suitable length of material 51 mm (2 in) wide, fold over, sew down one side, turn inside out and sew down the same side again. Insert the elastic under tension, turn in each end of the tube and sew in place, securing the elastic. Sew each end to inside of cape where required.

8
Making a 'Cricket-bag' Rucksack

One disadvantage with the rucksack is that very often the item required is at the bottom, and it is necessary to turn over the contents to find it. True, the rucksack can be packed systematically, but often in the course of a walk, unless the contents are tight, odd items can work their way down.

Time can be taken opening the rucksack and the retaining cord which gathers the neck has to be unknotted and also the straps can swell with damp, making it difficult to pull them through the buckles.

The handy backpacker can construct the 'cricket-bag' type rucksack shown in Fig. 8.1, quite easily. It is perhaps more useful for the solo-backpacker than members of a party. Single walkers will know definitely what they intend to carry, while a party of backpackers may have a miscellaneous collection of items which may be difficult to sort out and stow away satisfactorily.

The advantage of this rucksack is that all items of equipment are set out in compartments. In camp, the rucksack is laid on the floor and unzipped, and the backpacker should be able to put his hand on the required items without having to turn over a lot of kit.

If the backpacker intends to use the collapsible frame described in Chapter 5, this rucksack can be attached to it with elastic 'spiders', allowing a quick release and attachment when in camp. During the walk, the rucksack could be covered by the waterproof cape which would protect it from the weather and prevent any rain running in through the zip. If an anorak is worn, a plastic bag could be pulled over the rucksack to protect it.

Many walkers find that the best position for carrying a rucksack is high up between the shoulder blades and just below the neck. The difficulty is to get the load in just the right position; if it is too high on a frame, it can unbalance the walker when he is getting through a hedge; alternatively, if it is too low, it can tend to pull the shoulders down.

When designing the rucksack, the maker should arrange for the heavier weights to be placed in compartments which will be against this area between the shoulder blades. These items will usually be food and cooking equipment. Lighter, more bulky items like the rolled-up sleeping bag, can be stuffed at the bottom of the rucksack.

When the rucksack is attached to the frame, the load-retaining cord should be pulled tight round the load so that the compartments containing the heaviest weights are close to the back between the shoulder blades and just under the neck.

Some people feel that the ideal way to carry a load is without a frame and as close to the spine as possible; the weight then being well distributed and balanced in relation to the body. This is a matter of choice, as a rucksack carried close to the body can trap in the perspiration and there is the possibility of chilling when the rucksack is removed.

The maker who would like to try this method of carrying this rucksack is recommended to obtain a set of ex-military webbing cross belts and belt. Usually, these have ammunition pouches attached which can be adapted to carry small items of equipment or food where they are immediately available. Large D-rings will have to be sewn on the shoulders of the straps and on the sides of the waist belt for attaching the rucksack.

It is not practical to use the elastic 'spiders' for attachment. Two buckled straps must be made to pass round the rucksack and two leads sewn to them each side as shown. The four leads should terminate in a hook or strong dog lead clip (Fig. 8.1(a)). The load can then be unhooked rapidly from the carrying harness.

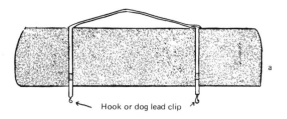

a

← Hook or dog lead clip

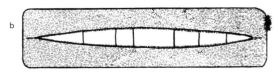

b

Cross-section Oval or round

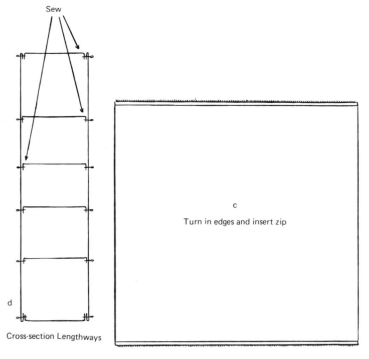

Sew

c

Turn in edges and insert zip

d

Cross-section Lengthways

Fig. 8.1   'Cricket-bag' rucksack.

When the backpacker travels by car or train, the harness or frame can be a nuisance, so accommodation should be arranged in the bag to take the harness or dismantled frame. If required, a removable carrying handle can be clipped to the two buckled straps (Fig. 8.1(a)) (used with the harness) or if the frame is used, straps and a handle could be made up.

The rucksack should be made of substantial material; tent canvas is probably the best and can usually be obtained locally from camping shops. Like most of the equipment described previously, the size will depend on the equipment and food the backpacker intends to carry. The bag should not be too long, or the top can catch on low branches, or the bottom on stiles and fences when the backpacker is getting over. Perhaps 762 mm ($2\frac{1}{2}$ ft) is a useful size for the average person. The narrower the width the better, and the maker will have to lay out equipment to obtain the best arrangements of compartments. The zip must be a substantial metal one, plastic ones are not strong enough. Use button-hole thread on the sewing machine with a large needle; as before, practice on scrap bits until the right tension is obtained. Use a medium stitch, fastening the ends securely.

The cross section of the rucksack can either be oval or round (Fig. 8.1(b)) but is at the discretion of the maker and depends on the bulk of the load. Allowing for seams, cut out the cross sections and ends and the outer cover. Put in the zip fastener first, turning in the edge of material as described in the chapter on tent making (Fig. 8.1(c)). Start at one end and sew in the cross sections and, finally, the other end (Fig. 8.1(d)). It may be necessary to leave part of the cross section seams open each side of the zip to allow sufficient room (Fig. 8.1(b)). Check carefully that all ends are secured, otherwise the seams may come apart at an inconvenient moment.

9
Canteens, Cooking and Cookers

Those contemplating backpacking must reconcile themselves to the fact that they cannot expect home cooking, or even the standard of cooking available on a static camp site. The importance of lightness necessitates a restricted menu if the backpacker is to keep his load within reasonable limits. Meals must be quickly and easily prepared and be satisfying. It should be possible to replace the food at village shops so the backpacker must consider traditional kinds of foods as well as the quickly prepared meals that are available at some supermarkets.

Foods and Meals

Frying is a messy business for the backpacker and should be avoided whenever possible. With their open air existence many walkers have a craving for fried foods. Farms will sometimes supply a hearty meal of bacon and eggs for the hungry camper, which can save a lot of messy washing up. If frying is undertaken it should be well away from the tent and equipment to avoid retaining that 'fried' smell and damage caused by the spilling of fat.

The backpacker must consider what alternative there is to potatoes and bread, impractical foods for the lightweight walker. If instant potato is satisfying, this could be used, or some would prefer the quick-cook porridge oats. One should consider rolled oats seriously. It is quickly prepared and the addition of different kinds of tinned meats can make a satisfying meal. The vegetarian could add a couple of eggs and some herbs to give the meal an appealing taste.

The most convenient kind of breakfast for the backpacker is probably a muesli of some kind. The base can be raw quick-cook porridge oats to which is added a handful of raisins, skinned peanuts and a compact cereal. The whole is wetted with dried milk and water and eaten with half an apple. This can be followed with two crispbreads, buttered if required. A large mug of tea finishes off the meal.

Walkers often find that they do not get very hungry during the day, so it is better not to eat too much, as this can tend to slow down the pace. Little and often is a good rule. Chocolate bars and glucose tablets are useful in-between snacks. Lunch can be two crispbreads and a piece of cheese with a drink of water. People who don't like drinking water can add lemon or orange crystals.

When the backpacker is tired at night, he does not want to waste a lot of time cooking a meal. A well organised meal can only take ten minutes to prepare, and is described at the end of the chapter.

Cooking Gear

Having decided on the kind of diet, the backpacker has to consider the type of cooker to use. It is not really practical to use a wood fire; the sparks fly about and can damage the tent; it is sometimes difficult to light and there is always the danger hazard. Solid tablet or liquid fuel cookers are available which are far more convenient than a wood fire.

The main consideration with any kind of cooker is the availability of fuel. Petrol is difficult to obtain in small quantities; camping gas cylinders are not always obtainable in remote country districts—a spare must be carried and the writer has found cylinders have a habit of running out unexpectedly. The solid fuel tablet form of cooker can only be replenished at camping shops (Fig. 9.1(a)). Methylated spirits is available at most chemists and paraffin could be obtained in small quantities from an obliging country ironmonger.

It would seem, then that the most suitable type of cooker would be one using paraffin or meths, providing it is light to carry, efficient and easily lit.

The small pressure stove is very efficient (Fig. 9.1(b)). In fact, it is possible to cook a three-course meal on it, keeping everything hot by careful arrangement of the pans. It is quite economical, but it can be awkward to light until one has had some practice. It is relatively heavy too, and unless one is prepared to make a special box for it (Fig. 9.1(c)), fuel can leak into the rucksack. This cooker is probably most useful for a party of three or more backpackers.

Fig. 9.1   A selection of cooking gear: (a) solid fuel cooker; (b) paraffin pressure stove, with (c) box and lid; (d) spirit stove with lid.

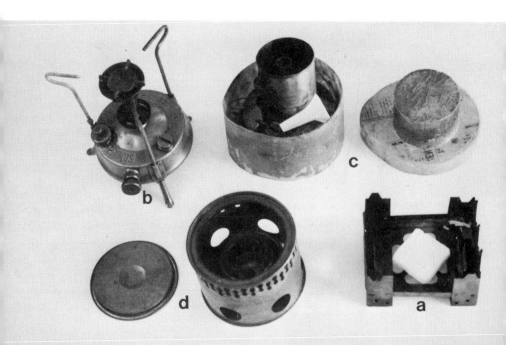

There are a few methylated spirit cookers on the market and a lightweight one (Fig. 9.1(d)) should not be despised, as it is easy to light, efficient, and the fuel is clean. Bottles containing 500 ml (17½ fl. oz) of methylated spirit are available from chemists and for two campers, one bottle should last four days (excluding the first day's breakfast), if they are following the menu previously set out. If one uses this kind of stove, it is a mistake to fill the container up to the level marked, if that amount of fuel is not going to be used. The most economical way of using the stove is to first pour the fuel into an aluminium container marked with a scale of 14.32 ml (½ fl. oz) up to say 114.56 ml (4 fl. oz). 43 ml approximately (1½ fl. ozs) should be sufficient to make two large cups of tea and provide washing-up water. 86.25 ml (3 fl. ozs) should be sufficient to make the tea, hot meal and washing-up water. When the container is filled with 43 ml (1½ fl. oz) of methylated spirits difficulty may be experienced in lighting the stove. A lighted strip of paper in the meths should set it burning. The snuffer on the stove can be dispensed with as the fuel will burn out on its own.

The solid fuel tablets can be carried as an emergency supply to use in the 'Express' stove, if required. With shears, cut out the centre stand of the solid fuel cooker so that it can be placed inside the 'Express' stove, which has had the spirit burner removed. Space should be allowed under the tablet to encourage a draught. The tablets can often deposit smoke on the pans, but they are useful in an emergency. Weight for weight, they have more or less the same heat output as the methylated spirits. Petrol, meths and paraffin should always be kept in leakproof metal screw-topped containers for safety, and marked to show contents.

Canteens

If the one or two backpackers intend to have the menu suggested, they will need a suitable canteen for cooking. The 'Jura' canteen is a useful purchase to adapt for two persons (Fig. 9.2). It consists

57

Fig. 9.2 The canteen and its contents: (a) large pan, (b) frying pan cover, (c) three metal plates, (d) two plastic cups, (e) additional large pan, (f) scouring pad, (g) stiff brush and towel, (h) two spoons, (i) water carrier, (j) salt, (k) pan holder, (l) plastic foam mat.

of one large pan with a frying pan-type cover: inside are three metal plates and two metal mugs, together with lifting handle. The metal mugs may be found to be unsatisfactory, as they burn the lips when filled with hot liquid. They can be replaced satisfactorily with two large plastic replacement cups for vacuum flasks. These can be made to nest closer by cutting back the handle of one of them at the base; they should then fit snugly in the canteen.

The three aluminium plates are very useful as food does not easily spill out of them. One of these plates can be enlarged round the edges by tapping progressively round the edge with a hammer and resting the edge against a piece of wood. It will then serve as a top for the additional large container which must be purchased separately.

The backpacker will need to search through the shops to find a lightweight aluminium saucepan which will fit inside the large pan of the 'Jura' canteen. The saucepan handle can then be removed and the holes hammered until they are closed. There will then be no possibility of leakage. The rim of the saucepan may need to be lowered to enable it to fit correctly inside the canteen.

The canteen will now consist of two large containers, a frying pan top, three metal plates, one enlarged, two plastic mugs and an aluminium lifting handle for the pans.

Inside the canteen the backpacker can carry a steel wool scouring pad and stiff brush for washing up, a small towel for drying the articles and two cranked spoons for eating the food. Spoons only are used for eating, and it is necessary to bend them so that they will fit in the canteen.

Cooking Arrangements

Tea for breakfast is made in a large container. Pour approximately 43 ml ($1\frac{1}{2}$ fl. oz) of methylated spirits into the stove burner, ignite it with a slip of paper and place on it the pan with about half a litre or a pint of water in it. Place the frying pan on top, add tea bag when boiling, and boil for a few seconds; remove from the stove and replace with an aluminium plate with a small quantity of water in it for washing up. The burner flame should die away, leaving the water hot.

When cooking the evening meal (Fig. 9.3) everything should be arranged beforehand, to save fuel. Pour about 85 ml (3 fl. oz) of spirit into the cooker; ignite, place the large pan containing a half litre or a pint of water on the cooker, cover with the plate or frying pan top; when the water is boiling, throw in a handful of quick cook porridge oats; wait approximately thirty seconds, then add previously chopped corned beef. Leave for a few seconds, remove, and replace immediately with the large pan containing water for tea. Cover, and while the tea water is heating, eat supper. Make the tea, remove the pan and replace with a small quantity of washing-up water in the frying pan. Leave the burner to die away.

To prepare eggs, tea and porridge at the same time, light the

59

Fig. 9.3 The evening meal set out with (a) water on cooker, (b) tea water and tea bag, (c) rolled oats.

cooker and place upon it the smaller pan containing the tea water.

Put the quick-cook porridge oats and water into the larger pan, and cover with the inverted frypan.

Place the large pan on top of the small one, and wait until the tea water is boiling. Meanwhile, wash and scrub the eggs.

Put the eggs into the tea water and replace large pan. After three minutes, add a teabag, again replacing large pan. Leave it for another minute, remove the eggs and tea, and place the porridge on stove to complete cooking. Wrap the eggs in a cardigan or jersey for insulation.

Remove the porridge and replace the tea (to stay hot) with the frypan containing washing up water on top.

This is the general procedure for two persons. One person may require less food and tea, so the amount of fuel can be adjusted to suit the circumstances.

Groups of three or more will have to purchase their cooking equipment to suit the size of the group. The paraffin pressure stove is probably better for the large group as it is more efficient than the spirit cooker for cooking large quantities of food.

To make the box for the pressure stove (Fig. 9.1) follow the general procedure for glassfibre work as described in Chapter 5. Make the bottom part of the box first. The box mould is made of cardboard and stuck together with adhesive tape. Grease the inside and lay on the mat and resin; only single mat is necessary.

When hard, trim the top edge, tear away the cardboard and grease the top outside edge. Make a cardboard lid which is shaped to accommodate the cooker central standard and condensed milk tin flame guard (Fig. 9.1(c)). Lay on the glassfibre mat and resin. When hardened, tear away the cardboard, place on top of the box and make the lip of mat and resin.

Leave it to harden and pull off the lid. Trim it and rub down with sandpaper, painting if necessary. A small plastic funnel is useful for this cooker, and disposable polythene gloves can be used when handling it so as to prevent the spread of the paraffin odour.

It is always advisable to cook *outside* the tent as the stoves and solid fuel cookers give off fumes—and there is always the possibility of the tent catching fire!

10
General Hints

Other Equipment

A *whistle* is a most important part of the equipment, (Fig. 10.1(a)). It is useful if any member of the party should become lost or it can be used to summon help in case of accident or illness.

A length of *nylon cord* should always be carried to replace broken or lost guys; to help hold down the tent in severe weather; to replace a broken bootlace; or even to serve as a belt to hold up trousers

Scissors are not absolutely essential, but they are useful for cutting nails and hair.

The *electric battery razor* is a time-saving item of equipment for the backpacker who shaves. It is most inconvenient to use a normal razor and soap in the confines of a small tent. The razor shown (Fig. 10.1(b)) has two cutting heads and is supplied in a soft carrying pouch with a cleaning brush. It takes four HP7 batteries Fig. 10.1(d) which should last four weeks, shaving every day. The batteries can be used in the torch described below.

This is a small light *plastic torch* which takes two HP7 batteries. The four razor batteries can be used in alternate pairs so that the amount of use from all the batteries is more or less even. It is advisable to carry a spare bulb in case the existing one fails.

At the time of writing it is possible to obtain a short *air bed and pillow* ('Li-Lo') weighing just under 0.7 kg ($1\frac{1}{2}$ lb) which is

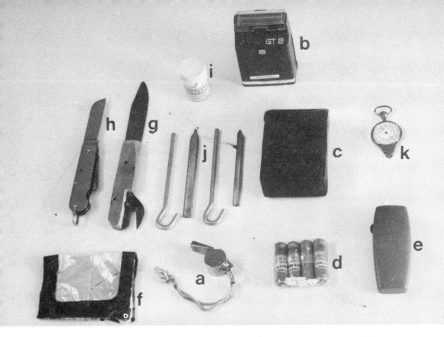

Fig. 10.1 Miscellaneous equipment: (a) whistle, (b) battery razor, (c) razor case, (d) batteries, (e) torch, (f) first-aid dressings, (g) and (h) knives, (i) water purifying tablets, (j) bamboo and alloy pegs, (k) map measurer.

useable with a down sleeping bag. It raises the sleeper above the cold floor, but it should not be inflated too much as there can be a tendency to roll off in the night!

A piece of *plastic foam* 356 × 432 mm (14 × 17 in) is useful (Fig. 9.2). It is warm to sit on in the tent or outside during a rest period. At night, it can form an extension to the air bed and makes it just that little bit longer and helps to keep the feet warm. During the walk, it can be bent round and inserted in the back of the rucksack to present a warm and comfortable surface to the back of the walker. It also protects one from the odd protruding items being carried.

Some kind of *water carrier* is necessary in camp and for carrying a small quantity of water for drinking during the day's walk. Plastic is the best material, it is light and strong. There are two types of carrier—rigid and collapsible. Collapsible carriers can be difficult to stand up, and when they contain water they are really not suitable to stuff into a rucksack, in case they may be punctured by some sharp object. A rigid container (which can often be purchased containing orange cordial) is better for packing in the rucksack, but it can take up a lot of room. Water can be carried safely, and it should stand well with little chance of being knocked over (Fig. 9.2). With careful husbanding, water requirements for two persons for a night's camp is about 4½ litres (1 gallon).

A *small towel* is necessary and it should be one which can be washed when dirty and dried as one walks along by tying onto the rucksack. *Soap* sufficient for washing, and soaping the socks can be carried in a plastic bag.

A *bowl* can be made from the bottom of a large plastic bag—or failing that—a circle can be cut from proofed nylon and an edge sewn round it as shown (Fig. 10.2). The water holds the bowl in shape, or it can be supported with stones or placed in a hollow in the ground.

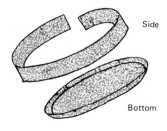

Side

Bottom

Fig. 10.2   Details of the nylon bowl.

Bowl

First aid requirements are a matter of choice—some people carry only adhesive dressings (Fig. 10.1(f)).

If two backpackers are together, and one is carrying the rucksack and the other the sleeping bags and rolled-up tent, then *spare clothes* can be carried in a *proofed nylon tube* in the centre of the roll. The tube is useful because it can be placed in between the airbeds at night to increase their area. Also, the tube can be laid on wet ground without the contents becoming damp. The size of the tube depends on the amount of spare clothing taken: the length should be the same as the width of the sleeping bags. This tube can soon be run up on the sewing machine, using a run and fell seam, and the entrance closed with a draw cord.

64

Toothpaste can last a long time, so to save weight the backpacker would be wise to take a tube that has been almost used up. This can be carried in a plastic bag with the toothbrush.

The *knife* is an important part of the equipment. The one shown (Fig. 10.1(g)) was adapted for use with a tin opener head. Two holes were drilled in the handle which has a wooden hand-grip one side. The other knife (Fig. 10.1(h)) is a military type dis-covered in the local government surplus stores. It carries a good tin opener, is sturdy, and can be carried by a lanyard or cord suspended from the belt. It is then available for immediate use. The *tin opener* is a most important accessory: so many 'camping knives' have such a variety of gadgets on them, but no tin opener.

One great difficulty for the backpacker is finding pure water to drink. This snag can be overcome by carrying *water-purifying tablets* (Fig. 10.1(i)). One of the tablets is added to 1 litre (1¾ pints) of water and set aside for ten minutes before use. Greater quanti-ties of water require a longer time, and two tablets should be used

Fig. 10.3 The 'Filopur' water filter.

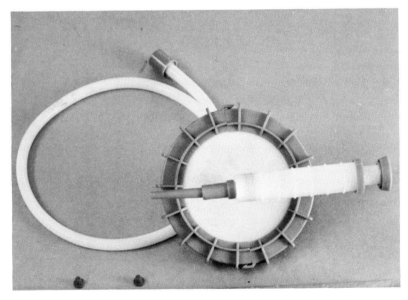

65

when the water is from a heavily contaminated source. The manufacturer's instructions should be followed at all times. The *lightweight filter* shown in Fig. 10.3 is useful. When using this filter, the intake plastic hose is attached to one side of the 'Filopur' medium container. The plastic pump is fitted to the other side of the container and the intake is dipped into the water supply and the pump manipulated. The 'Filopur' filter can possibly produce more drinking water in ten minutes than the purifying tablets, but it weighs considerably more. The filter medium, too, has to be replaced after about 100–400 litres of filopurized water have been supplied. If you wish to be fully independent, you could choose either of these ways of ensuring a supply of drinking water.

A *camera* is worth carrying in order to record the experiences of the backpacker.

Some cameras are quite heavy, but it should be possible to buy one—probably a 35 mm model—which would weigh less than 224 g (8 ozs), including the film.

Binoculars are heavy, and for the backpacker are they really worth while? Interesting though it may be, one does not really have too much time for watching wild life. A lightweight monocular or telescope (say 10 × 25) is useful to see distant signposts or to determine one's position. The figures 10 × 25 indicate the power (10) and the light gathering capacity of the glass (25). Many telescopes have high magnification and relatively low light gathering capacity, so that it is difficult to see through them in poor light. A 10 × 25 telescope is a reasonable compromise, can be obtained cheaply, and is light and a useful addition to the equipment.

Needless to say, a *toilet roll*, or part of one is an absolute necessity. If no farm site toilet is available and it is necessary to defecate in the countryside, a hole should be scraped in the ground and the excrement and paper covered over with the loose soil and pressed down. It is offensive to other walkers to leave the area in a disgusting state, and moreover, the excrement attracts flies.

Insects can be a nuisance to the backpacker during the summer season. Oil of Citronella is a useful deterrent to these pests. The oil has a pleasant aroma and should be rubbed over the hands and hair: in course of time the odour diminishes and the oil has to be replaced.

The backpacker should have little trouble with bees; they are usually anxious to be off about their business. Sometimes, however, they are attracted by bright clothes or the sweat on the backpacker, and they settle on him. One can usually take a deep breath and puff them off, or flick them away quickly with the forefinger strained against the thumb. If a bee is brushed off, it might sting and this sting can be left in the wound together with the poison sac. The sting should be eased out carefully with a finger nail, taking care not to squeeze the sac.

Wasps can be a great nuisance during the summer months. Like bees, they are curious and can be attracted by colour and odour. People who are allergic to insect bites and stings should carry the appropriate antidote or seek immediate medical aid when stung or bitten. When eating food care should be taken that a wasp has not settled on it before placing it in the mouth, as a sting can be serious or fatal.

If the backpacker wears a brimmed hat, corks on lengths of string can be fixed around the brim to keep away insects. A handkerchief stuffed in the back of the cap and allowed to flutter free is a great help. With these aids and the Citronella, the backpacker should keep the insects at bay. However, look out for wasp's nests, which are usually in holes in the ground or bankside. Keep well away from the nests as the angry occupants can rush out and cause serious injury.

When setting up camp at night, the tent should not be pitched under trees as sometimes a branch can fall off for no apparent reason: the backpacker should also carefully scrutinise the ground to see if he may be pitching his tent on an ant's nest. These insects can be a real nuisance, invading the tent in search of sugar granules or sweetness of some kind. Their bite can be quite sharp, and being so small are difficult to evict. The backpacker can take a small tube of some proprietary make of anti-insect bite ointment if he wishes.

In the Countryside

Cows are usually inoffensive creatures and are often curious about the backpacker, bounding up to him, hoping that he has something to eat. Bulls can be dangerous, and if one is on the footpath, it is futile to argue about rights-of-way. Discretion is the better part of valour, and the field should be avoided. Horses and ponies may look endearing, but they can have nasty little ways about them. They can stand on one's feet, take a crafty bite at an elbow, or turn round and kick.

Many townspeople and urban dwellers do not realise that the countryside is not just a place for the pleasure seeker, but represents the farmer's workplace, his way of life. His stock-in-trade is the contents of the fields, growing crops or livestock, and he is justifiably annoyed if any damage is caused by thoughtless people straying across growing corn or leaving gates open, enabling the animals to roam about.

There is heavy pressure on the countryside as an amenity, and the visitor should show consideration to the farmer by behaving correctly when he is there. With a little thought, a good relationship between farmer and visitor could be maintained.

Bad conduct by visitors to the countryside can be reflected back upon the backpacker when asking a farmer if one can camp for the night. Permission could be refused, or an exorbitant charge made by the resentful farmer. In such a situation, the backpacker should use diplomacy, and talk to the farmer, attempt to mollify him and try and encourage a good relationship. Most farmers should respond to the suggestion that all visitors to the countryside are not the same, and so will meet the backpacker 'half-way'.

The land everywhere belongs to someone, so the owner should be sought out and permission obtained before camping. Often, farmers will supply eggs and milk which can form a useful addition to the menu. Fires should not be lighted without permission; after all it is the farmer's wood that is burning, and it is very important that all fires should be kept under proper control. Camp sites should be left clean and tidy, and all litter taken home.

Health Points

Carrying a heavier than usual rucksack can affect the feet of even the most seasoned rambler. With the extra pressure, the feet can become sore, blistered and chafed. The hardy walkers push a needle and cotton through their blisters and cut off the cotton so that a piece passes through both holes, the liquid oozes out and the blister is not so painful. Such a practice is not really to be recommended as it could cause infection and really the best way of avoiding foot trouble is to prevent it beforehand. The feet should be prepared for at least two weeks before setting out on an expedition. The most satisfactory way is to rub them night and morning with surgical spirit or methylated spirits to harden them off. After the first hour or two of backpacking, the feet may become painful. The walker should stop, take off boots and socks and rub the feet with meths, applying it with cotton wool. It is advisable to repeat the process at frequent intervals during the day, and if possible bathe the feet in cold water. It should be found that the feet will require less and less attention during the following days, as they become used to the exercise and weight.

It is a mistake to keep on walking all day without adequate rests; the body eventually becomes fatigued and the backpacker begins to feel that he can go no further. A more sensible idea is to have a ten-minute rest in every hour. The rucksack can be removed and the body can relax. It is surprising what a difference this regular rest makes. One can face the walk again with renewed vigour, and it is only late in the evening when one can begin to feel really tired.

Map Reading

It is most important that backpackers should know their position

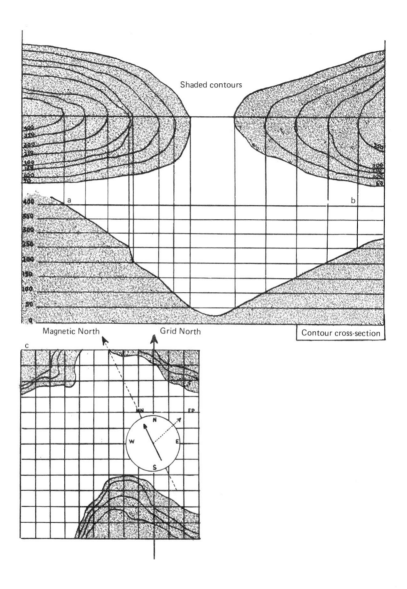

Fig. 10.4 Basic elements of map reading, with interpretation of contour lines.

in the countryside at all times. To the town dweller, the country-side can be a bewildering place of large open spaces, with no signs to indicate ones position. Accurate map reading, then, is a most essential skill. The three main maps used by the backpacker are the Ordnance Survey 1 : 250000 series (two-and-a-half inches to the mile), the old 1 : 63360 series (one-inch-to-the-mile), and the new 1 : 50000 series (two-centimetres-to-the-kilometre). (These scales mean that two-and-a-half inches on the map represent one mile on the ground : one inch on the map represents one mile on the ground, and two centimetres on the map represent one kilometre on the ground, respectively). The map is flat and the surface of the ground is irregular, so that it is not possible to produce a perfectly accurate map. A reference panel is given on the smaller scale maps, and one can be obtained for the two-and-a-half-inch map. The reference panel shows signs and symbols used on the map to indicate such objects as churches, post offices, rights-of-way, etc.

The height of various parts of the landscape is indicated by contours (Fig. 10.4(a)). A contour is a line drawn through places of the same height above sea level and the height is shown in small numbers on the contour. The contour interval—that is, the vertical interval—is the vertical distance between contours. Where the contours are close together, the slope is steep; where they are far apart, the slope is gentle (Fig. 10.4(b)). It is essential, when planning a walk in unfamiliar terrain, to consider the contours carefully, or the backpacker might find the going harder than he expected.

The Ordnance Survey Maps are set out in numbered squares called the grid reference. This helps one to refer to a specific point on the map. The necessary instructions on how to do this are incorporated with the map reference panel.

To enable the backpacker to find his way in strange country, a *compass* is a necessity (Fig. 10.5). When buying a compass it is important to check that the needle does not swing about a great deal before settling down. This can be most irritating, especially when one has to stand in an exposed spot in the pouring rain waiting for the needle to cease swinging! On some compasses the needle can stick and give a misleading bearing. The writer has found the 'Silva' compass accurate, reliable and lightweight. A device called the tachometer can be attached to it for counting the number of steps taken, should the walker wish to be very accurate with his compass work.

A compass needle points along the *magnetic* north-south line. On most maps the magnetic north symbol is shown and the compass should be placed over this symbol and the map turned about until the direction of the compass needle and the symbol coincide. The map is then set in correct relationship with the landscape. It will be observed that the needle does not point to true north, so that allowance must be made for this when determining the direction in which to proceed, or to find one's position on the map. This difference between true and magnetic north or south is called the *magnetic variation*, and changes slightly from year to year. It will be noticed on the map that grid north is also indicated; so that altogether we have three 'norths'—magnetic, true and grid. One way of using the compass is to set the right or left-hand edge against the north-south grid line, and turn the map until the magnetic north and grid north are in the correct relationship. This saves unfolding all of the map, which is carried in a clear plastic envelope to protect it from the rain.

Fig. 10.5   Three types of compass.

The compass rim is numbered in degrees—360 to a full circle. This can be moved round until the letter N coincides with grid north. The compass is now set and by looking at the map, the backpacker can see the direction in which to walk (Fig. 10.4(c)). It is true that grid north and true north are not really the same, but one should not experience any difficulty in this matter. Perhaps the footpath lies 47° east (Fig. 10.4(c)). Holding the compass in the hand, the needle and grid north always being in the same relationship, walk in that direction until you strike the footpath.

You should know your position at all times, by making a habit of checking by map and compass at frequent intervals. This is very important, particularly in hilly or mountainous country, where few distinguishing features can be observed.

The sun can be a useful indicator of the correct direction, and the landscape should be observed and objects mentally recorded, so that if it is necessary to retrace one's steps, the path can be better recalled.

Distance can be estimated by the time taken to walk a given distance and it is sensible to find out one's particular rate of walking before setting out on an expedition. Allowance should also be made for the type of terrain.

The backpacker who is keenly interested in map reading and compass work may like to know more about *orienteering*. This is a sport requiring the competitors to find their way to a given point by map and compass in strange country in the shortest possible time. Information on this subject can probably be found at the local public library.

Planning a Walk

The backpacker, experienced in static camping and fully organised and equipped for his first adventure, must consider where he is going to go. Again, a public library is useful for information about the long-distance footpaths or rambling routes in the countryside. However, you may like to plan your own walk, using the Ordnance Survey maps showing the foot and bridle paths which are Rights of Way. Perhaps you would like to start off with a four-day expedition. If you have a car, where will you leave it? Where will you obtain supplies of food and where will you camp? Obviously, a circular route is the most suitable, returning to the car. The car can be left at a farm and the farmer would expect some payment for this privilege. The first day's walk should not be too far to allow time for the car journey. Walking on succeeding days could be progressively longer, or shorter, according to the backpacker's inclination. These early outings are voyages of discovery. The backpacker is finding out his capabilities.

Village Post Offices are indicated on the map, and often food can be purchased there, but don't depend on them, as they may be Post Offices only and have no provision shop attached. Local knowledge is always the best, and country people can advise the backpacker if there is a food store in the next village or hamlet.

Public libraries have lists of camping sites and several published lists are also available at newsagents and book shops. Go through them all, as some sites can be listed in one book and not in another. Usually, the lists give information about the services available, if any, and one can plan accordingly. Before setting out, it is advisable to telephone the chosen site owners to see if they are still taking campers.

List of Suppliers

Sleeping Bags, Fillings, Nylon, etc.
'Pointfive', Banton & Co. Ltd., Meadow Lane, Nottingham
  NG2 3HP

Materials, Zips, Threads, Velcro, Fillings
Pennine Boats, Hard Knott, Holmbridge, Huddersfield, West
  Yorkshire HD7 1NT

Tents, Sleeping Bags, Clothing and General
Blacks of Greenock, P.O. Box 6, Port Glasgow, Scotland PA14
  5XN

Tents, Sleeping Bags, Jackets, etc.
Fjällräven, H. A. & J. M. McLaren (Agencies), Markington,
  Harrogate, North Yorkshire HG3 3NR

General
Mountaineering Activities Ltd., Wellington Mills, Duke Street,
  Manchester M3 4NF

Tents, Capes, etc.
Robert Saunders (Chigwell) Ltd., Five Oaks Lane, Chigwell,
  Essex 1G7 4QP

Glassfibre suppliers are listed in the 'yellow pages' of local telephone
directories. Also, motor vehicle accessory suppliers sometimes
stock this material.

Index